**ABDO** Publishing Company

# Stay Fit

GET HEALTHY

A Buddy Book by **Sarah Tieck**

## VISIT US AT
www.abdopublishing.com

Published by ABDO Publishing Company, PO Box 398166, Minneapolis, MN 55439.

Copyright © 2012 by Abdo Consulting Group, Inc. International copyrights reserved in all countries. No part of this book may be reproduced in any form without written permission from the publisher. Buddy Books™ is a trademark and logo of ABDO Publishing Company.

Printed in the United States of America, North Mankato, Minnesota.
102011
012012

 PRINTED ON RECYCLED PAPER

Coordinating Series Editor: Rochelle Baltzer
Contributing Editors: Megan M. Gunderson, BreAnn Rumsch, Marcia Zappa
Graphic Design: Jenny Christensen
Cover Photograph: *iStockphoto*: ©iStockphoto.com/ArtmannWitte.
Interior Photographs/Illustrations: *AP Photo*: John Amis (p. 7), Mark Baker (p. 19); *Getty Images*: Kevin Mazur/WireImage (p. 7); *Eighth Street Studio* (pp. 21, 26); *iStockphoto*: ©iStockphoto.com/andipantz (p. 13), ©iStockphoto.com/barsik (p. 11), ©iStockphoto.com/comotion_design (p. 11), ©iStockphoto.com/Eraxion (p. 11), ©iStockphoto.com/Erdosain (p. 30), ©iStockphoto.com/forestpath (p. 27), ©iStockphoto.com/ktaylora (p. 30), ©iStockphoto.com/Mik122 (p. 13), ©iStockphoto.com/monkeybusinessimages (p. 5), ©iStockphoto.com/numbeos (p. 23), ©iStockphoto.com/pixdeluxe (pp. 9, 15), ©iStockphoto.com/Rubberball (p. 17), ©iStockphoto.com/Thomas_EyeDesign (p. 23); *Photo Researchers, Inc.*: Gustoimages (p. 25); *Photolibrary*: Superstock (p. 19); *Shutterstock*: Benis Araporic (p. 9), Elena Elisseera (p. 9), Golden Pixels LLC (p. 26), Gorilla (p. 27), Rob Marmion (p. 25), Morgan Lane Photography (p. 29), Jiri Paulik (p. 17).

## Library of Congress Cataloging-in-Publication Data

Tieck, Sarah, 1976-
  Stay fit / Sarah Tieck.
    p. cm. -- (Get healthy)
  ISBN 978-1-61783-236-9
  1. Physical fitness--Juvenile literature. 2. Exercise--Juvenile literature. I. Title.
  GV481.T55 2012
  613.7--dc23
                                        2011030934

# Table of Contents

Healthy Living ................................. 4
Movers and Shakers ....................... 6
Let's Get Physical .......................... 10
Pump You Up! ................................ 14
Move That Body ............................. 16
Train, Train, Train .......................... 18
Look and Learn ............................. 20
Now and Later ............................... 22
Brain Food ..................................... 26
Making Healthy Choices ............... 28
Healthy Body Files ........................ 30
Important Words ........................... 31
Web Sites ...................................... 31
Index .............................................. 32

# Healthy Living

Your body is amazing! It does thousands of things each day. It lets you smile, jump, and think. A healthy body helps you feel good and live well.

In order to be healthy, you must take care of your body. One way to do this is to stay fit. So, let's learn more about exercise and fitness!

Staying fit gives you energy and helps you become strong.

# Movers and Shakers

You can move your body in many different ways. Some kids bike or walk to school. Others play in parks or at recess. Activities in gym class or after-school sports also get you moving.

Movement of all kinds is healthy. But, the best kind gets your heart beating faster. It works your lungs and other body parts.

In 2010, First Lady Michelle Obama presented Let's Move. This campaign works to help kids become more active.

In 2011, singer Beyoncé helped teach kids about movement. She showed them that dancing is a good way to stay fit.

People exercise to stay fit. When you exercise, you sweat and breathe hard and fast. Your **muscles** may feel tired. This means your body is working hard!

Regular exercise is good for your health. It prevents sickness. It makes you more **flexible**. And, it helps you stay at a healthy body weight.

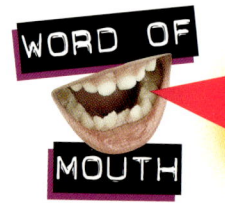

**WORD OF MOUTH**

After you work out, be sure to wash your body. Sweaty skin can smell bad!

Some people exercise in groups or as part of a team. Others exercise alone.

# Let's Get Physical

Exercise makes you stronger inside and out! **Aerobic** exercise makes your lungs and heart work hard to get **oxygen** to your body. This type of exercise includes jumping rope, dancing, and playing soccer.

lungs

Jogging is an aerobic exercise. It makes your heart and lungs stronger.

heart

11

Other exercises mostly work your **muscles**. When you lift something heavy, your muscles work to move it. Over time, they get stronger and can lift more weight. Climbing and doing push-ups are ways to build muscle.

Exercises that strengthen your muscles also make your bones stronger!

# Pump You Up!

Exercise doesn't just make you stronger. It affects your mood, too. When you work out, your body lets out **chemicals**. They make you feel happier! You may also feel full of **energy**. You may even learn better in school!

Exercise affects your thoughts and feelings as well as your body.

# Move That Body

You can move your body anywhere! Many people plan activities or use special **equipment**. This can help push them to work their bodies harder.

Some people join a sports team or go to a gym. Many walk outside with their dogs. Others exercise with DVDs at home. You could even grab some hula hoops and have a contest with friends!

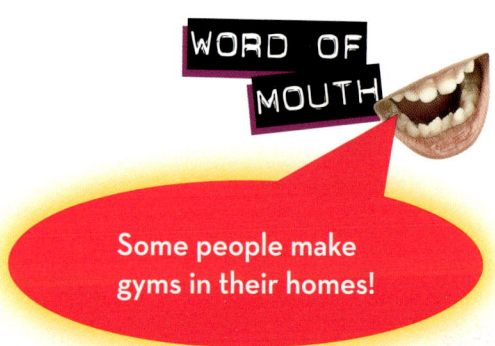

WORD OF MOUTH

Some people make gyms in their homes!

People plan fitness activities depending on the weather. On warm summer days, they may run through sprinklers. During cold winter months, people enjoy skiing.

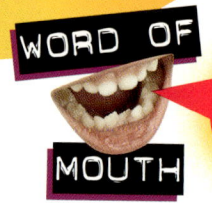

Proper shoes and clothes protect your body during a workout.

# Train, Train, Train

Many people play sports on a team. Others take part in individual sports, such as swimming or running. They are all called athletes.

Athletes train for their sport. They practice their skills. And, they do other workouts to grow stronger.

**How It Sounds**

athlete (ATH-leet)

Swimmer Michael Phelps spends many hours practicing in a pool. He also stretches, lifts weights, and exercises outside the pool. This makes him an even better swimmer.

There are athletes of all shapes, sizes, and abilities. Basketball and tennis (*right*) are common sports for athletes in wheelchairs.

# Look and Learn

How do you know if you are working out hard enough? Some people just pay attention to how their bodies feel.

Others measure their heart rate. This is the number of times your heart beats per minute. A tool called a heart rate monitor measures this. You can also find this on your own by counting heartbeats.

**WORD OF MOUTH**

To find your heart rate, place your fingers on your wrist or neck. Count the number of beats in 60 seconds!

# Exercise Scale

### 9–10
You are breathing hard, sweating, or can't talk. You are working out very hard! Most people can only do this for a short time.

### 7–8
You can talk a little, but it is hard to sing. You are pushing your body to move.

### 5–6
You are moving with purpose, but it isn't too hard.

### 3–4
You are not sitting. But the movement you are doing is very easy, like when you wash dishes.

### 1–2
You are sitting and your body is at rest. Your breathing is slow and normal, so it is easy to talk and sing.

# Now and Later

Do you like to watch TV or spend time on a computer? These activities require a lot of sitting. Make sure you're also doing things that get you moving.

If you aren't moving enough, your body may get tired and out of breath easily. Even small, slow movements can be hard.

When you don't exercise enough, you may lack energy. This can make it hard to pay attention during school.

In addition to fitness, it is important to eat the right amount of food. If you eat more than your body needs, you may gain weight.

Over time, not exercising enough can lead to health problems. Your bones and **muscles** may get weak. You might get less **flexible**. You could also become overweight.

Regular exercise helps prevent serious health problems later in life. These include heart problems and **diabetes**. Make good choices now to keep your body healthy for many years!

Staying fit helps keep your bones strong as you grow older.

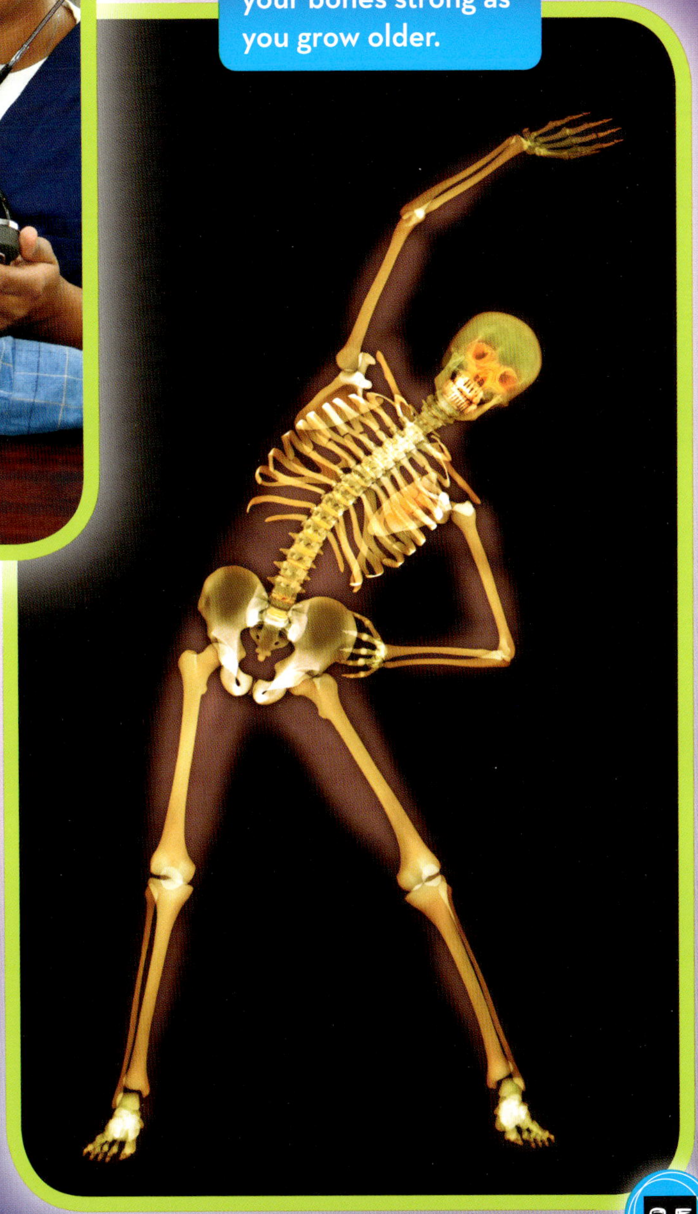

Regular exercise helps keep your heart healthy.

# Brain Food

**I don't like exercising with other people. What can I do instead of team sports?**

There are many ways to be active besides playing team sports. You could go for a nature walk or play a video game that gets you moving. If you find a type of exercise that is fun, it won't feel like work!

## How do you know how much is enough exercise?

Every person needs different amounts of exercise. The amount depends on how much you eat and other things. Scientists say children should exercise for 60 minutes each day. So, move a little whenever you can.

## I want to lose weight. Can exercise help?

When food taken in is not useful to the body, the extra calories may be stored as fat. Exercise is one way to use it up.

# Making Healthy Choices

Remember that exercise makes your body stronger. Move as often as you can. When you choose to be active, you make your body healthier.

Fitness is just one part of a healthy life. Each positive choice you make will help you stay healthy!

Your school may have fitness equipment on the playground and in the gym.

# HEALTHY BODY FILES

## BODY FUEL

✔ Eggs, cheese, and meat help you build **muscles**.

✔ Apples or pasta can give your body a boost before a workout.

## PLAY IT SAFE

✔ Warm up with light movements before an activity.

✔ Stretch after working out so your muscles don't get sore. Regular stretching will make you more **flexible**, too!

## DRINK UP

✔ When you sweat, your body gets thirsty. So, drink lots of water before, during, and after a workout.

✔ Water plays an important part in helping your body build muscle. So, drink up!

# Important Words

**aerobic** (ehr-OH-bihk) relating to exercise that increases oxygen in the body and makes the heart better able to use oxygen.

**chemical** (KEH-mih-kuhl) a substance that can cause reactions and changes.

**diabetes** (deye-uh-BEE-teez) a condition in which the body cannot properly take in normal amounts of sugar and starch.

**energy** (EH-nuhr-jee) the power or ability to do things.

**equipment** (ih-KWIHP-muhnt) supplies necessary for a service or action.

**flexible** able to bend or move easily.

**muscle** (MUH-suhl) body tissue, or layers of cells, that helps move the body.

**oxygen** a colorless gas that humans and animals need to breathe.

# Web Sites

To learn more about staying fit, visit ABDO Publishing Company online. Web sites about staying fit are featured on our Book Links page. These links are routinely monitored and updated to provide the most current information available.

www.abdopublishing.com

# Index

aerobic exercise **10, 11**

athletes **18, 19**

Beyoncé **7**

bones **13, 24, 25**

diabetes **24**

energy **5, 14, 23**

flexibility **8, 24, 30**

food **23, 27, 30**

health problems **8, 24**

heart **6, 10, 11, 20, 24, 25**

heart rate **20**

Let's Move campaign **7**

lungs **6, 10, 11**

mood **14, 15**

muscles **8, 12, 13, 24, 30**

Obama, Michelle **7**

Phelps, Michael **19**

sports **6, 9, 10, 11, 16, 17, 18, 19, 26**

stretching **19, 30**

sweat **8, 21, 30**

water **30**

weight **8, 23, 24, 27**